The Vampire Library

Encounters
with Vampires

DAVID ROBSON

ReferencePoint
Press®

San Diego, CA

About the Author

David Robson's many books for young people include *The Murder of Emmett Till*, *The Israeli-Palestinian Conflict*, and *The Devil.* He is also an award-winning playwright whose work for the stage has been performed across the country and abroad. Robson lives with his family in Wilmington, Delaware.

©2011 ReferencePoint Press, Inc.

For more information, contact:
ReferencePoint Press, Inc.
PO Box 27779
San Diego, CA 92198
www.ReferencePointPress.com

Picture credits:
Cover: iStockphoto.com
AP Images: 10, 39, 63, 65
iStockphoto.com: 6, 31, 34, 72
North Wind: 23
Photofest: 17
Photoshot: 50
Science Photo Library: 60

Series design and book layout:
Amy Stirnkorb

LIBRARY OF CONGRESS CATALOGING-IN-PUBLICATION DATA

Robson, David, 1966-
  Encounters with vampires / by David Robson.
      p. cm. -- (Vampire library)
  Includes bibliographical references and index.
  ISBN-13: 978-1-60152-133-0 (hardback)
  ISBN-10: 1-60152-133-2 (hardback)
  1. Vampires. I. Title.
  BF1556.R63 2011
  398'.45--dc22

                                                        2010010100

Contents

Introduction: "Vampires Will Always Be with Us"   4

Chapter 1: Searching for Clues   8

Chapter 2: Vampire Sightings   21

Chapter 3: Vampire Attacks   33

Chapter 4: Vampire Hunters   47

Chapter 5: Vampire Imitators   61

Source Notes   74

For Further Exploration   76

Index   77

Introduction

"Vampires Will Always Be with Us"

Few have escaped their clutches. Most instead have fallen under their spell and willingly surrendered to the bite of the vampire. Not literally, of course, but through books, movies, and folklore, the lure of vampires remains as strong as ever.

The bloodsucker of yore may have been popularized by Bram Stoker in his 1897 novel *Dracula*, but that classic tale was not the first story of a ghoulish, bloodthirsty creature who stalked the night searching for fresh flesh to sink his teeth into. The legend of the vampire goes back thousands of years. Native American tribes told of a vampire-like monster with a trumpet-shaped mouth that sucked out the brains of its victims. In Greece storytellers spoke of alluring vampire women—the children of Hecate, the goddess of witchcraft— who feasted on the blood of their male victims. Bulgaria's *ustrel* is a child born on a Saturday that dies in infancy and then returns to dine on small animals. The ancient Chinese were encouraged to bury their deceased quickly, in fear that unless they did so, a vampire-like creature might result. They referred to these vampires as *kiang shi* or *chiang shih*.

Over the centuries the appearance of vampires evolved. No longer godlike, nor completely monstrous in appearance, the fanged fiend appeared—at least in shape and size—human. But looks deceived, masking the vampire's superior strength, mind-control abilities, and power to transform itself into other creatures, most notoriously a bat. Before long, too, vampire stories became less the stuff of legends and folktales; instead journalists around the world began reporting about real-life encounters with mysterious, rarely seen beings who stalked the night in search of fresh, life-giving blood. People were told how to avoid becoming victims of these merciless brutes and how yelping dogs, hissing cats, and neighing horses might serve as warning signs of the presence of a vampire.

Despite the circumstantial evidence, scholars and scientists long ago rejected the notion of vampirism. Instead, they say, folktales, mythology, and even reports of real vampires provided a way by which people might cope with strange, unexplainable occurrences. In a time in which little was understood about virus and disease, stories of vampires, werewolves, zombies, and other macabre creatures helped provide a sense of stability and control over the invisible forces that surrounded people.

In the twenty-first century, a fascination with all things vampire persists. It can be seen most recently in the enormously popular Twilight series of novels by Stephenie Meyer and the subsequent movie versions, or on the television program *True Blood*. These works of fiction, written to excite the imaginations of teens, never purport to be anything more

Strange as It Sounds...

A Kenyan blood cult known as the Mau Mau killed and drank the blood of over 2,000 people in the 1940s and 1950s.

One of the world's largest bats, a grey-headed flying fox, takes flight. Vampires have often been described as having exceptional strength, the power of mind control, and the ability to transform into other creatures—most notably bats.

than fantasy. Yet even today evidence suggests that vampires may not simply be the stuff of fiction. Contemporary newspaper accounts attest to a stark reality: There are people who literally drink blood, either for fun or in dark, sinister rituals. Many who claim to be vampires are no more than disturbed individuals who call themselves vampires because it makes them feel, or appear, more commanding than they truly are. Others are members of vampire communities. These groups reject violence, lead otherwise ordinary lives, and obtain their required blood not from helpless victims but from willing volunteers.

Vampires, in other words, are both fictional and real. But drawing a line between the supernatural vampire and its all-too-human counterpart is not always an easy task. The encounters themselves suggest that the truth about vampirism remains as elusive as the lonely phantom itself, flying high above the city, desperately seeking a bloody feast before retiring to its creaky coffin. Whether they are real or fictional, author Neil Gaiman says that vampires and the questions surrounding them will never disappear: "Whether as metaphor or as something else—something that stirs the blood, makes you dream of immortality and night, that rustles the counterpanes, or just leaves you glancing nervously at a locked door, because after all, they can move as mist—vampires will always be with us."[1]

Chapter 1

Searching for Clues

Cultures from ancient Mesopotamia to modern China have searched for clues that might prove the existence of the phantomlike creatures known as vampires. Early tales were passed from village to village, striking mortal fear into the hearts of populations both large and small.

Much of the evidence for or against the existence of vampires has been lost in the whirligig of time. But what is clear is that in a more primitive age, what began as a rumor quickly passed into belief, and superstition often became truth. In the twenty-first century, evidence of vampirism is rare but not unheard of.

Feasting on Animal Blood

Although most reports of vampires go back generations, Puerto Rico's chupacabra first appeared in the 1990s. Unlike the fictional tales of vampires, the chupacabra is not one of the undead—in fact, it was never human to begin with. Instead the chupacabra—which combines the Spanish words for "suck" and "goat"—refers to a creature described this way by Puerto Rican construction worker Luis Guadalupe: "It was about four or five feet tall and had huge elongated red eyes. A pointy, long tongue came in and out of his mouth. It was gray but his back changed colors. It was a monster."[2]

The first evidence of a creature that devours goats, cows, pigs, and other livestock occurred in Puerto Rico in 1995, when 8 sheep were found slaughtered. Each animal had 3 puncture wounds and had been drained of blood. In the months and years that followed, other countries—Mexico, Chile, Argentina, El Salvador, Brazil, and the Dominican Republic—turned up similar proof of the bloodthirsty chupacabra. In July 2004 ranchers claimed that chupacabra-like creatures killed their livestock in Texas. More bloodsuckers were reported in Russia in 2006. This time the vampire killed and drained 32 turkeys.

A 2007 Texas study of the mysterious animal killings strongly suggested the presence of a coyote, not a chupacabra. Scientists remain skeptical about the existence of vampires and chupacabras. Hector J. Garcia, the former head of the U.S. Department of Agriculture's veterinary services of Puerto Rico, says, "We can speculate forever, but I haven't found anything that would make me doubt that we're searching for something that we can define. Those famous fangs that suck blood I've yet to see. Maybe the result of all this is to expose the need for better control of stray dogs and animals."[3]

José Soto, former mayor of the Puerto Rican city of Canóvanas, remains most concerned about the safety of citizens. "Whatever it is, it's highly intelligent," he said. "Today it is attacking animals, but tomorrow it may attack people."[4]

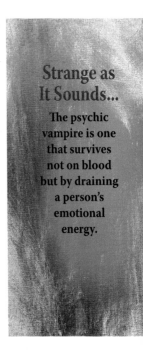

Strange as It Sounds...
The psychic vampire is one that survives not on blood but by draining a person's emotional energy.

Signs of Death (and Life)

Dead cattle aside, proof of vampires can be difficult to come by. The folklore and mythology surrounding the fanged

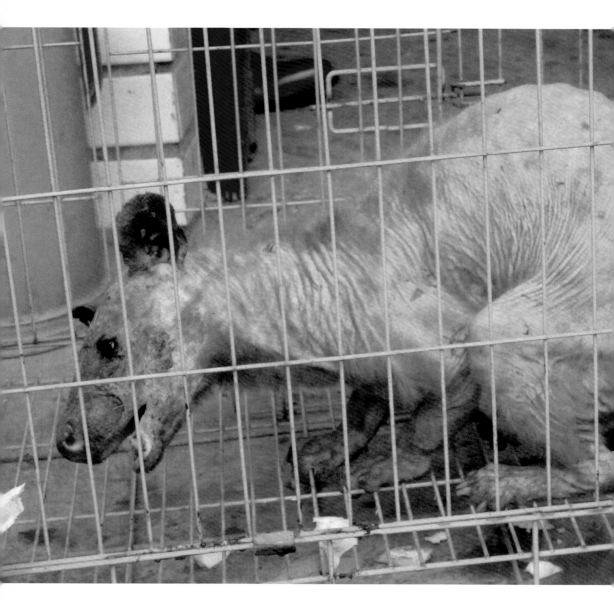

Attacks by bloodthirsty chupacabras have been reported in countries around the world. In China in 2010 villagers captured a mysterious creature (pictured) that was attacking chickens. A Chinese newspaper described it as a chupacabra.

fiends offers clues to the vampires' behavior, but physical evidence that the undead actually roam the earth feasting on the blood of their victims is often disputed or even laughed at by experts. Still, those who claim to have been terrorized by the strange creatures say it is no laughing matter.

The story of Hungarian soldier Arnold Paole became infamous in the first half of the eighteenth century. After returning home from war, Paole told villagers a story of how he had been victimized by a Turkish vampire he met during the war in Serbia. To avoid becoming a vampire himself, Paole told the locals that he had found the vampire's grave and eaten some of the soil in which the vampire was buried. Afterward he dug up the beast and rubbed himself with its blood. This, he believed, would prevent him from turning into a vampire.

One investigator at the time described a vampire in this way: "A vampire is a body that in all respects appears to be dead except that it does not decay as we expect, its blood does not coagulate, and it may show changes in dimension and color."[5]

But only weeks after returning home from war, Paole was accidentally killed when a cartload of hay fell on him. One month later four villagers were found dead with bite marks on their necks. The town's mayor ordered an immediate exhumation to see if Paole had indeed become a vampire. As suspected, 40 days after Paole's death, decay had not set in. His body, engorged with blood, showed the traditional signs of the undead. "His body was flushed," according to folklorist Raymond T. McNally, "his hair, nails, and beard had grown, and his veins were full of liquid blood."[6]

Temple of the Vampire

Those looking for evidence of real vampires—of the self-proclaimed variety, at least—need look no further than the Temple of the Vampire. Billing itself as an ancient religion, the group promises members eternal life. Vampires, the temple says, are predators, separated from humanity by a desire to feast on mortals. "The Temple of the Vampire . . . can enable you to acquire authentic power over others, build real wealth, achieve vibrant health, and even live beyond the usual human lifespan," according to its Web site. This is done by joining and working toward certain levels in the vampire hierarchy. First a fledgling immortal must become a lifetime member by donating money to the temple. After applying and gaining an official acceptance letter, the active member can develop his or her supernatural powers and advance to the level of vampire predator. This can eventually lead to advancement to the level of vampire priest or priestess. Members learn the ways of darkness by studying the temple-published *Vampire Bible*. Critics of the group label it a scam, a method by which its owners collect money from the curious and the gullible.

Temple of the Vampire, "If Vampires Were Real, Would You Want to Be One?" 2010. www.vampiretemple.com.

Local Superstition

The disturbing case of Paole is not unique. In seventeenth-century Slovenia, in an area known as Carniola, peasants told tales of the undead haunting their waking hours. One such instance occurred when a beloved and respected local farmer named Grando died. His reputation for hard work and kindness brought people from all over Carniola to his funeral. But in the days after the funeral, a number of villagers became the victims of a mysterious, bloodthirsty monster.

Town elders met and decided that the creature who terrorized them could only be Grando. They begged the church for permission to exhume, or dig up, the body; they received it. Soon after, a small group made its way to the local cemetery, found Grando's grave, and began digging. After nearly an hour, their shovels struck wood. Two men jumped in the grave and helped lift the pine box out of the crypt. Town leaders pried off the coffin lid and were stunned by what they saw. Weeks had passed since Grando's death, but the corpse was lifelike, as if the deceased were only sleeping. "The complexion was ruddy like that of a man alive," wrote McNally. "His face quivered, then curled into a cruel grin, taking in a breath of new air. His eyes popped open."[7] Those present began to pray. This, they believed, was the mark of a vampire.

Drained of Strength

Another piece of evidence that suggests the presence of a vampire is the fatigued feeling that victims describe. In July 1910 a British magazine called the *Occult Review* published an account that led some readers to suspect vampirism.

English diplomats stationed in India began feeling ill. The first victim requested transfer to another position, and as his condition worsened he was granted the transfer. The official's health improved. Months later others began getting sick, only to recover when they left the area.

Then a medical officer's wife began to suffer from similar symptoms of fatigue and depression. She knew no cause, until she awoke one night from a nightmare, screaming. She told her husband that in her dream she saw a creature in the room—a cross between a giant spider and a jellyfish. Although her husband tried to soothe her fears, day by day she lost strength and her pulse weakened. It was as if her life was melting away. Before it was too late, the woman insisted she return home to England. Instead she and her husband left for a vacation. Miraculously the woman's health improved. But upon their return to India, her depression and weakness returned.

One night she told her husband to examine her neck and shoulders. "See if there is any mark on the skin or any kind whatever," she said. "See if you can find any puncture from a sharp-pointed tooth."[8] Despite his careful study, her concerned spouse found no evidence of any tooth marks. The wife's explanation for the examination was simple: In another dream a man grabbed her, put his mouth to her neck, and drank. "I felt that he was drawing all the blood and life out of me,"[9] she said. The vampire then cast her aside, and she lost consciousness.

A day or two later, as she and her husband ate dinner, the wife noticed a tall, wealthy Indian man across from them. Her blood ran cold. This was the man from the dream. Her husband confronted the man, who soon after disappeared and was never seen or heard from again.

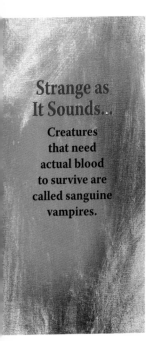

Strange as It Sounds...

Creatures that need actual blood to survive are called sanguine vampires.

Creepy Count Vardalek

Another vampire story, difficult to verify, occurred in Austria in the early eighteenth century. One night a wealthy man invited a guest he had met on the train to stay with him. The guest, Count Vardalek, claimed to be from Hungary. Vardalek spoke languages—German, Polish, and French— and astounded his host with his knowledge of history. In the initial account of Vardalek's visit, he is described as snakelike and pale.

The count's age was difficult to guess, but he at first appeared to be in late middle age. After arriving at his host's home, Vardalek settled into his room before joining the host and his family for dinner. When he descended the stairs to greet his hosts, the count appeared greatly changed: "He looked much younger," reported the host's daughter. "There was an elasticity of the skin, combined with a delicate complexion, rarely to be found in a man."[10] Before long, one of the grown children named Eric became entranced by the count— as if in the count's power. In the days that followed, Eric and Vardalek grew closer, often speaking together privately, shunning other members of the family. But as the weeks passed, Eric gradually became sick. His complexion grew pale, and he often took to his bed, unable to rise. Family members saw that Eric was dying, but they were baffled as to the cause of his illness. As Eric grew weaker and death seemed imminent, the family called a local Catholic priest to the house to administer last rites. By the time the clergyman arrived, Eric lay dead, and Vardalek had vanished.

The Last North American Vampire

In late-nineteenth-century New England, belief in vampirism was at its peak. The fear among citizens was so great that

Strange as It Sounds...

Dousing a vampire with holy water will burn it.

*OPPOSITE:
Untreated,
tuberculosis
ravages the
body. In this
state, one ex-
pert says, a
person might
resemble
the German
film vampire
Nosferatu—
a pale,
gaunt, sickly
looking being
with dark,
sunken eyes
and protrud-
ing teeth and
ears.*

the *New York World* newspaper reported on it. At least six documented incidents of supposed vampirism occurred in Newport, Rhode Island. According to folklorist Michael E. Bell, "This generally occurred when several members of the same family appeared to die from a similar wasting disease." Residents, wrote Bell, "believed that a vampire fed first on those it was close to before moving on to other people."[11] Thus it appeared that the first victim was transformed into a vampire and then feasted on its family members.

Such was the case with 19-year-old Mercy Brown, a farmer's daughter who died of tuberculosis in 1892. In the days and weeks after her burial in Chestnut Hill Cemetery, her brother Edwin became sick. His strength greatly diminished, and before long he began looking scrawny. His body appeared to be wasting away. The residents of tiny Exeter, Rhode Island, suspected vampirism, and 2 months after her burial, town officials exhumed Mercy's body, searching for clues. One account of the disinterment claims that Mercy's body had turned over in its grave. Her corpse was flushed with what observers believed to be fresh blood, so officials cut out Mercy's heart, burned it on a nearby rock, and fed the ashes to Edwin in hopes that he would recover his strength. He did not; instead he died 2 months later.

Such evidence holds little validity, say contemporary historians and scientists. In all likelihood, says Bell, the tuberculosis, also known as consumption, killed Edwin Brown, as it had his two sisters and his mother before him. According to Bell, a person with tuberculosis looks "the way vampires have always been portrayed in folklore—like walking corpses, which is what you are, at least in the later stages of consumption. Skin and bones, fingernails are long and curved, you look like the vampire from [the 1922 movie] *Nosferatu*."[12]

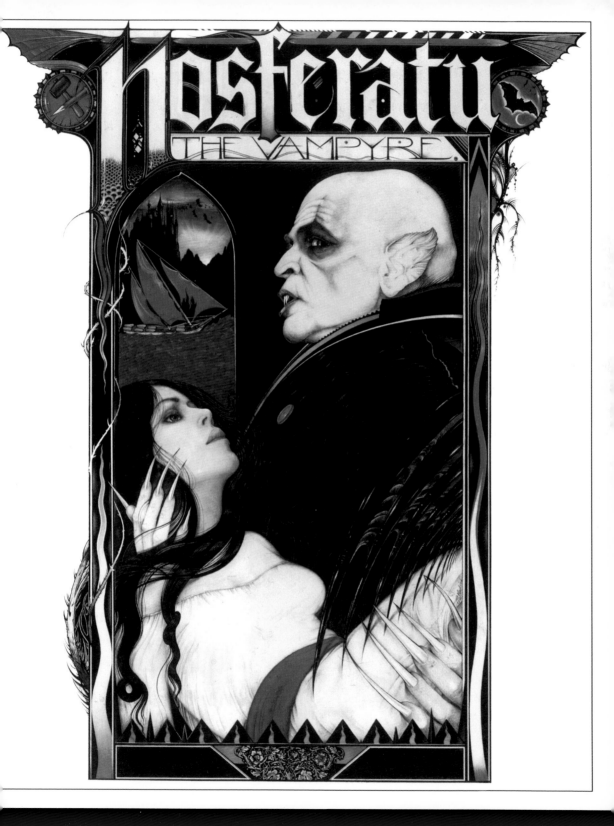

Illness in communities was often blamed on supernatural forces because of a limited understanding of the body's processes. If Mercy Brown did turn over in her grave, there is a simple explanation. Before the regular use of embalming, in which the body's fluids are replaced with chemicals to preserve the corpse, cadavers were known to move around involuntarily in their coffins. Mercy's legend grew because her community had no other explanation. "She basically absorbs the ignorance, the fears, and in some cases the guilt that people have," said Bell, "because their neighbors, friends, and family are dying, and they don't understand why and they can't stop it."[13]

The Vampire Disease

In addition to consumption, doctors have long compared vampirism and its symptoms to rabies: desperate thirst, hypersensitivity to odors and lights, muscle spasms, and animalistic behavior. But in recent years contemporary science has offered another logical explanation for the behavior commonly referred to as vampirism.

In the mid-1980s University of British Columbia biochemist David H. Dolphin performed pioneering work in the field of porphyria diseases. Such ailments occur when the body cannot produce important chemicals naturally. The result: Sufferers find their skin ultrasensitive to light. In the worst cases the skin becomes brittle and disfigured; the nose and fingers can drop off, and lips and gums shrivel, causing the teeth to jut out and look menacing, even fang-like. According to Dolphin, 1 in every 200,000 people may have the disease. Although no cure for porphyria disease exists, a blood by-product called heme is used to treat symptoms. Dolphin has deduced that during the Middle Ages,

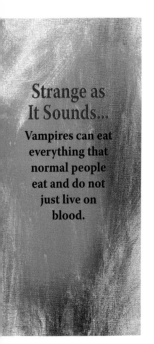

Beware of the Langsuyar

Perhaps the most terrifying creature in all of Southeast Asian folklore is the langsuyar, a vampire-like being found in the stories of Malaysia. The first langsuyar was a beautiful woman who gave birth to a stillborn child. Upon learning of her baby's death, the woman clapped her hands three times, lifted off the ground, and flew into a tall tree. From then on, Malaysians spoke of seeing the long-haired woman wearing a green robe. The ankle-length hair concealed a hole in her neck through which she sucked up the blood of newborn children. According to legend, women who died in childbirth, or within 40 days after, were in danger of becoming langsuyars. In an effort to prevent such a transformation, family members typically placed glass beads in the mouth of the dead woman. Eggs were put under her arms to discourage flying, and a needle was inserted into each of her hands to prevent her from attacking others. When these methods failed, the langsuyar could be trapped and captured by clipping her long hair and nails and jamming them into the hole in her neck.

porphyria sufferers might have felt the urge to drink blood as a way of curing their malady. "It is our contention," said Dolphin, "that blood drinking vampires were in fact victims of porphyria trying to alleviate the symptoms of the dreadful disease."[14]

The lethal bite of the vampire—often passed from one sibling to another—may have passed into legend because the gene for porphyria might have been shared in families, even if only one member showed symptoms of the disease. "If that victim then bit a sibling to get blood," wrote journalist Philip M. Boffey, "the shock of the experience might have triggered an attack of the disease in the bitten sibling, thus producing another vampire."[15] In the eighteenth century the British royal family apparently suffered from the disease. Its most famous victim, King George III, eventually died in madness.

As for garlic, thought to be a useful item for driving away vampires, Dolphin surmised that because the vegetable contains chemicals that make the symptoms of porphyria worse, those ill with the disease had a biochemical dislike of it. But porphyria sufferers are not vampires. Their unusual genetic condition only provided an excuse to a public that did not understand such disorders.

The Realm of the Undead

Misunderstanding and superstition are often at the root of alleged vampire encounters. The clues that lead some to believe that vampires exist are typically viewed by skeptics as having logical, earthly explanations. But what of the incidents that seem to defy explanation? Though traditional methods of investigation may suggest otherwise, believers cite these unexplainable encounters as evidence of a realm populated by the undead.

Chapter 2

Vampire Sightings

Those who claim to have seen vampires often doubt the occurrence, or they allow friends and family to convince them that they should not trust their senses. Still, others remain firm in their convictions, relying on intuition and instinct, feelings in the pit of the stomach that defy a logical, or even sensory, explanation. These witnesses insist that they have indeed been in the presence of vampires, as unbelievable as such episodes may seem. And, they say, the experience is one they will take with them to their graves.

The Count de Saint-Germain Refuses to Die

According to legend, vampires are immortal, meaning they do not die. Only by destroying them will they cease to exist. By this criterion, the Count de Saint-Germain was clearly a vampire. Fluent in Greek, Arabic, Chinese, English, Italian, and a handful of other languages, the count traveled the world in the late 1700s, billing himself as a master alchemist—a person believed to have the power to transform base metals into gold. He also painted with colors so vibrant and lifelike that other painters envied his paint-mixing ability and believed he had supernatural powers.

Yet the count's most mysterious and fascinating quality was his deep knowledge of history. When he spoke of the

Strange as It Sounds...

In 2000, 800 animals were reported slaughtered by chupacabras in Chile.

OPPOSITE:
*Jesus turns wa-
ter into wine in
this painting
depicting the
marriage feast
at Cana. In
the 1700s, long
after the event,
the Count de
Saint-Germain
described
the feast as if
he had been
present. His
extraordinary
knowledge of
history and
other quali-
ties convinced
some that he
was a vampire.*

past, listeners sat enraptured. He made it sound as if he had witnessed the events of which he spoke, including the marriage feast at Cana during which Jesus was said to have turned water into wine. He bragged about being more than 2,000 years old and could allegedly render himself invisible at will. His fountain of youth, he claimed, was a mysterious liquid that kept his skin from sagging, his bones from becoming brittle, and his health as that of a man in his twenties. While the count never revealed the secret of his alleged longevity, rumor suggests that he may have feasted on blood to retain his youthfulness.

Records suggest that Saint-Germain died in 1784, but five years later, during the French Revolution, he is thought to have reappeared. According to accounts of the time, in 1789 he sent a letter to Marie Antoinette, the doomed queen. The queen sent her aide, Madame Adhemar, to meet with the count in a nearby chapel. There the mystery man told the woman that his efforts at preventing the downfall of the monarchy had failed. Soon after, he disappeared again, never to return. Saint-Germain's legend only grew, but the question remains: Was he a vampire?

According to paranormal expert Brad Steiger, the count's vampire credentials are strong. Like many vampires, "He never stayed in any one place too long," writes Steiger. There-fore, he could not be easily connected to local murders. Also, "Many people went missing in those days . . . and persons of lower classes were often murdered by their superiors with-out suffering the consequences."[16] The deaths of servants or peasants were rarely investigated by authorities; the count, if he wished, could fulfill his blood lust and not fear being dis-covered. His wealth and status may have protected a man many suspected of being a vampire.

The Mystery of Croglin Grange

The evidence for Saint-Germain's vampirism remains circumstantial, but few reputed vampire sightings are as well-known as the one that took place in the hamlet of Croglin Grange in northwestern England in the mid to late nineteenth century. Although certain details of the case vary, including the precise year, most agree that sometime around 1875, the Fisher family decided to rent out their house in Croglin Grange. The family had lived on the property for hundreds of years, but they decided to find more spacious accommodations one year as the chill of winter set in.

At first the owners could find no tenants, but the blooming of spring attracted a young family of siblings. Amelia Cranswell and her two brothers, Michael and Edward, soon took up residence, delighting in the lovely, old house and the neighboring village whose people welcomed them with open arms.

By the time the first blush of spring had turned to summer, the three could not imagine ever leaving Croglin Grange because they felt so at home there. On warm evenings Amelia often took long walks through the churchyard that sat just across from the house, or she joined her brothers as they read on the porch. One night when the heat was stifling, Amelia decided to sleep by a large window in order to feel the evening breeze. In another account she was simply passing by the window. Nevertheless, upon gazing into the gloom, Amelia's eyes caught sight of two faint points of light rising above the darkened churchyard gravestones. More curious than frightened, she stayed fixed on the lights as they brightened and appeared to move closer, out of the cemetery, over the church wall, and onto the front lawn of the house. As if in a trance, Amelia sat frozen, watching the approaching beams grow larger. She shook herself as if to awaken, shut and bolted the window, and tried to calm down. Finally she turned from the window and fell into a restless sleep.

Shortly afterward Amelia heard a sound that began as a light tap on the window—like a tree branch bumping against the house in the wind—but soon became a scratching sound. She sat bolt upright, peered out the window, and saw two demonic eyes staring into her own. One of the small window panes shattered. A hand reached in, fumbled with the lock, and pushed open the window. The young woman screamed, but the hands were upon her, clutching at her throat. By now, Edward and Michael had burst into the room and beaten back their sister's attacker, which fled. Amelia lay unconscious but alive, with bite marks on her neck—the marks of a vampire.

After their horrifying ordeal, the Cranswells left Croglin Grange for Switzerland, but in time they returned. Their first spring back, the creature returned, too. One night the brothers found it skulking around the house. They chased it, firing on it with rifles and grazing its leg. When the fiend tried to escape, they followed it back to the churchyard, tracing the vampire to a grave. Not wanting to push their luck, Michael and Edward left and returned to the cemetery the next day with a group of locals. When they opened the grave, they found a corpse with a bullet wound in its leg. The group subsequently burned the corpse.

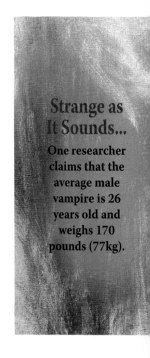

Strange as It Sounds... One researcher claims that the average male vampire is 26 years old and weighs 170 pounds (77kg).

Vampire in the Flesh

More than a century later, in 1979, an eight-year-old American girl named Lara sighted a vampire. Sick from a cold, she lay half awake in bed talking to her mother, who

Vampire Research Center

Steven Kaplan's interest in so-called real vampires began in the early 1970s. After a thorough investigation of the phenomenon, he determined that in 1972 there were at least 21 self-identified vampires living in the United States and Canada, some claiming to be 300 years old. Kaplan subsequently founded the Vampire Research Center in Elmhurst, New York. His investigation revealed a thriving but secretive vampire subculture in North America. Kaplan divided vampires into 3 categories. The first are those who are simply attracted sensually to blood. The second group contains imitators, who don capes, dress in black, and otherwise act out their fantasies based on fictional vampire tales. Third are those whom Kaplan deems "real." These creatures—humans all—seek blood to drink, believing it will fill them with energy and, perhaps, help them live longer. Most potentially dangerous, according to Kaplan, are those in the last category. Yet few, he believes, actually kill to obtain blood. Instead these "true" vampires find other ways to get what they think they need. In one case Kaplan noted a man who worked as a hospital technician so he could feast on stored blood whenever he needed it.

sat in bed beside her. Once the two settled in for the night, Lara's mother fell asleep, but Lara's stuffy nose and high fever made sleep difficult for the child. After tossing and turning for what seemed like hours, Lara suddenly saw a tall, attractive woman with long, flowing black hair standing on the right side of her bed. The woman's teeth were bared and pointy. Horrified and in fear, Lara sat immobilized. She shut her eyes tight, hoping that when she opened them the apparition would be gone. Even with her eyes closed, she could feel the terrifying presence of the vampire. Slowly Lara reached out and nudged her mother. "Mom, there's a vampire in the room," she whispered. "Mom. . . ."[17] Lara's mother only rolled over and told her to go back to sleep.

What occurred next is fuzzy in Lara's mind—she was very young. She thinks she again shut her eyes and tried to bury herself under the covers. She grabbed her mother's waist and prayed for deliverance from her worst-ever nightmare. Finally she fell asleep and awoke the next day feeling better but no less certain of what she had seen the night before.

The memory of the vampire woman remained with Lara, but as she got older she became less convinced of what she had seen, chalking the vision up to her high fever and cough medicine. Vampires do not exist, she told herself; logic overpowered her senses. She and her mother moved away, Lara graduated from high school, and she began her life as an adult. But at 23, Lara returned to the neighborhood in which she had grown up. She visited old friends and reminisced about old times, sitting on a park bench and enjoying the first breath of spring air.

After a time another friend, Ana, skated by on Rollerblades. Lara and Ana hugged. They had been next-door neighbors as children, and the young women exchanged phone numbers and promised to keep in touch. But before they parted, the conversation turned to ghosts, ghost stories, and strange happenings. Ana revealed that as a girl, she had once been visited by a tall, attractive woman with long, flowing black hair. Lara gasped. Ana went on to describe the woman's vampire-like teeth and frightening stare. Like Lara, Ana had been sick when she witnessed the strange figure. Living barely 10 yards (9m) away, they had both seen the same vampire and lived to tell about it.

Curious Behavior in a New York Hospital

In 1981 one of the most bizarre vampire sightings was reported in New York City, although its truth is difficult to verify. A middle-aged man was walking across Fifth Avenue when he was hit by a car. Luckily for him, an ambulance sat in traffic behind the spot where the accident took place. Medics quickly came to the man's aid. They saw no blood, and the man remained conscious, so they put him on a stretcher and loaded him into the ambulance for a drive to the nearest hospital. During the drive the injured man barely said a word; the medics described him as dazed and confused.

When they arrived at the hospital and doctors took a closer look, the patient, who had no identification on him, refused treatment. He would allow no X-rays nor intravenous medicine nor the taking of blood for testing. Instead he insisted he had to leave. The emergency room doctors refused to let him go; they wanted to keep him overnight for observation. Once he was ensconced in a private room, a nurse offered him food and something to drink. Again the man refused, only wanting to be left alone.

The next day the man received a visit from an elderly couple carrying large duffel bags. Later in the day a muscular

Vampire Hysteria

In the 1990s Iran's capital city was terrorized by a mysterious and terrifying killer that newspapers quickly dubbed the Tehran Vampire. For 3 months, beginning in March 1997, a man posing as a taxi driver stalked the night, luring women into his car to murder them. Unlike vampires of lore, Ali Reza Khoshruy Kuran Kordiyeh did not drink the blood of his victims; instead he killed them with wooden stakes. In an effort to destroy the evidence of his crimes, Kordiyeh then attempted to burn the bodies. The Tehran Vampire might have continued his killing spree, but two women who escaped went to the police. They told of a maniacal cab driver and provided physical descriptions of the man. After months of investigation, authorities tracked down Kordiyeh and found bloodstains inside his taxi. He confessed to his diabolical crimes soon after. By this time he had kidnapped and murdered nine girls and women aged 10 to 47. The vampire's execution took place on August 13, 1997. Iranian officials leaked news of the event to the press, and 10,000 people showed up to witness the hanging.

orderly came to the room with strict orders to take the man for X-rays. Rather than put up a fight, the man complied. Once he was gone, the nurse on duty entered the room. She had observed the man's curious behavior and now became curious herself. The duffel bags lay empty. She wondered what had been in them, and once she walked into the bathroom she found out: There, strewn on the floor, were piles of blood-donation bags, most of which were now empty. Confused, the nurse felt a surge of dread. She hurried out of the room into the hallway. There, sitting in the wheelchair, was the orderly, bite marks on his neck, the mysterious, blood-drinking man hovering over him. The nurse screamed, which brought a security guard running down the hall. Fangs bared, the angry vampire lunged at the guard, who fired two shots that seemed to have no effect. The vampire crashed through a window, fell 20 stories, and disappeared into the night.

In this account, as in so many other purported sightings of vampires, fact and fiction appear to coexist. Few people will admit to having seen a vampire, and those who do expect to be taken at their word. Yet witnesses are typically written off as deluded, dishonest, or mentally ill.

"He Had Fangs"

Carol, a 30-year-old living in the United States, does not consider herself mentally ill. Yet as a child of 8 or 9, she says she encountered a vampire-like creature at her bedroom window. One night as she and her little sister prepared for bed, they saw a man with black hair floating outside their window.

Frightened but fascinated, the girls stared at the man, who now put his hands against the glass. The phantom

In 1981, a nurse in New York City reported finding bags of donated blood, like the ones shown here, strewn across a hospital floor—most emptied of their precious contents. Moments later she encountered a patient, fangs bared, hovering over an orderly.

smiled. "He had a strange smile," Carol remembers, "and he had fangs."[18] Although the mysterious man never said a word, Carol said she could hear his voice in her head telling her to let him come in. But Carol and her sister pulled themselves away from the window and ran out of the room.

The vampire did not return until Carol grew up. And this time he appeared in a dream. In the dream a large bird flew into her bedroom, but once inside, it transformed itself into the same creature she and her sister had seen 20 years before. As the vampire stood, staring at her, Carol noticed two bite marks in his neck. She felt his power. Like before, he was silently calling to her, asking her to join him.

There the dream ended. But one night in September 2007, unable to sleep, Carol felt herself going into some sort of trance in which she stepped outside her own body. She watched from another part of her bedroom as her body rose from bed, walked to the window, and peered outside. On the ground below stood a black-haired figure wearing black clothing. When the creature saw Carol looking down at him, he immediately flew to her window, again asking for entry. Frightened but strangely curious, she cracked open the window. The vampire grabbed Carol's hands; she could feel his long fingernails on her skin. He had something for her, he said, an orange necklace and pendant that he would leave for her in a jewelry box. Then, before she could stop him, the vampire was in the room with her and the two of them were floating above her bed. The vampire kissed Carol before she blacked out.

Since then Carol has had more encounters with her vampire, usually in dreams. He tells her he does not want to harm her. "I don't know what he wants with me," she says. "I'm not afraid of him. I'm just curious and strangely allured to him."[19]

While some would argue that Carol has a very active imagination and is likely inventing her encounter with a vampire, believers in the supernatural would say that she has been very lucky. Although seduced by the vampire's mystery, she has lived to tell her tale. Those attacked by vampires are not always so fortunate.

Chapter 3

Vampire Attacks

While many investigators have tried, documenting actual cases of vampirism is nearly impossible. If vampires do exist, few of them are willing to be interviewed, preferring instead to live private lives far from the public eye. Still, if proof of the existence of vampires remains thin, a deep-seated fear of vampires persists among the general population. Stories—many at least partly based in fact—perpetuate the notion that all that happens in the world cannot be so easily explained. In fact, these tales—both ancient and contemporary—often defy logic and encourage more supernatural explanations.

Countess Bathory: Bloodthirsty Vampire

One historical figure whose mysterious life and disturbing behavior may have encouraged rumors of vampirism was Transylvania's Elizabeth Bathory. Born into an ancient and enormously wealthy family in 1560, young Elizabeth began having violent seizures at an early age. Today the child would likely be diagnosed as an epileptic. But in an age in which unusual medical conditions were barely understood and often believed to be brought on by demonic possession, Elizabeth's odd behavior frightened her family.

At 15, Bathory was married off to another royal, 26-year-old Hungarian count Ferenc Nadasdy, and took up residence at the Castle Cséjthe. The newlyweds were not together for long. The count was called off to war for long periods of time. In her husband's absence Bathory began dabbling in the occult after being introduced to it by a servant. Before long, Bathory herself was spending days or even weeks away from the castle, participating in dark rituals and cavorting with townspeople believed to be witches.

Once, she returned from an extended sojourn and was confronted by the count, himself recently returned. He bitterly scolded her for her disappearance, as did his demanding and abusive mother. Bathory's anger turned to cruelty as she, with the help of her former nurse, Ilona Joo, began torturing young servant girls. In an age when royalty often treated servants as slaves to be used as they wished, such behavior was not considered out of the ordinary. But Bathory's sadistic punishment went beyond mere discipline. "She did not just punish infringements on her rules," wrote vampire expert J. Gordon Melton, "but found excuses to inflict punishments and delighted in the torture and death of her victims far beyond what her contemporaries could accept."[20] Bathory's methods of torture included sticking her fingernails into sensitive parts of her servants' bodies. Punishment in the cold weather was equally harsh, as victims were stripped of their clothes and drenched with water until their bodies froze.

Bathed in Blood

Accounts vary as to whether the count involved himself in this torture. In some versions of the story, he taught his wife a number of brutal techniques; in others Bathory did not begin her assaults on others until after his death in 1604.

OPPOSITE: Consumed by a desire to remain young and beautiful, Elizabeth Bathory brutally killed scores of young women and then bathed in their blood. Her evil acts are said to have begun in Transylvania (pictured).

By then she had given birth to 4 children, 3 girls and a boy, and moved her family to Vienna. Motherhood did not soften her; instead widowhood and greater responsibility only increased her barbarity and bloodlust. Renowned not only for her cruelty but her staggering beauty, Bathory, over 40 by now, feared growing older. Once, when a servant girl mistakenly pulled her hair while brushing it, Bathory slapped the young woman, drawing blood. The droplets of red landed on Bathory's own hand, and after rubbing it in she became convinced it gave her skin a healthy glow. She ordered two male servants to kill the servant girl and drain her blood, after which Bathory bathed in it.

Thereafter, scores of young women were sacrificed for Bathory's blood baths. Little notice would have been taken had Bathory not overstepped the rules of propriety and murdered a noble woman like herself. Aided by local widow Erzsi Majorova, Bathory murdered a young royal in 1609 and tried hiding her deed by calling the death a suicide, but local authorities became suspicious. Before long, officials also learned of the disappearance of scores of young women who had worked in Bathory's house. Authorities could ignore the evidence no longer and promptly arrested the countess.

Her trial began in early January 1611. The key piece of evidence was a ledger in which Bathory had recorded the names of over 650 victims. In the end her accomplices were put to death, and Bathory herself was sentenced to life imprisonment in her castle. She was kept in solitary confinement in a room with neither doors nor windows; she died there on August 21, 1614. Elizabeth Bathory's bloody reign ended; her bloody deeds became legend. Her alleged vampirism has inspired countless books and movies but has never been proved.

Mexican Vampire

Early-nineteenth-century Mexico was likewise terrorized by a being alleged to be a vampire. Citizens of Guadalajara, in the west-central part of the country, began reporting dead livestock drained of blood and young mothers were horrified to find their newborns pale and lifeless. The city stayed on guard, and early one morning, just before daybreak, another vampire attack occurred. Soon after the attack, a witness spotted a strange-looking, disheveled man making his way back home. After alerting other townspeople, the witness led an angry mob toward the mystery man's house. Once there they broke down the door, attacked the suspect, and drove a stake through his heart.

Afterward they hastily buried the man they suspected of being El Vampiro in a local cemetery, El Panteon de Belen. According to local legend, the piece of wooden stake lodged in the dead man's heart soon grew thicker and in time became a tree that grew over the grave. Over decades the tree became larger until it cracked open the tomb of the dreaded vampire. Locals began saying that if a person cut a limb from the tree, blood would seep out. They prophesied that when the tree grew large enough to cover the grave completely, El Vampiro would return to wreak revenge on the people of Guadalajara.

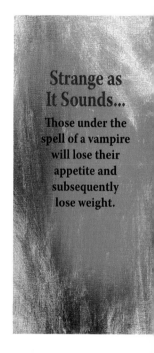

Strange as It Sounds...
Those under the spell of a vampire will lose their appetite and subsequently lose weight.

Maria's Encounter

More than a century later, a curious child named Maria played on the streets of Guadalajara. She especially loved exploring the cemetery at El Panteon de Belen, and each year on the Day of the Dead, she and her family spent hours there, walking among the graves and paying tribute to deceased relatives. Maria did not remember when she first heard the story of El Vampiro, but after she learned of the grisly tale, she made a point of visiting the cracked-open tomb as much as she could. At times she thought she saw something moving among the shadows near the grave, but her mother always laughed and told her it was simply her imagination. When she was 11 and old enough to visit the graveyard on her own, Maria immediately headed to the vampire's grave, moving in closer and peeking down into the cracked mound of hard dirt. She always made the trip during the day but once, near midnight, she crawled out of her bed, quietly crept out the back door, and walked the few blocks to El Panteon. She took a deep breath, swallowed her nervousness, and climbed the high cemetery wall.

Once inside she looked around for the caretaker, who usually roamed the grounds at night with his guard dog. She saw no one. Maria then made her way a short distance to El Vampiro's grave. Silence enveloped the place. She moved closer to the grave itself and again peered into the cracked crypt; in the moonlit darkness she could see little, so she used her hands to feel along the mouth of the broken tomb. She dropped her legs inside, thinking she would try to squeeze down into the pit. First she removed a small candle and lighter from her pocket. After lighting the candle, she crouched down and wiggled her way through the opening. Upon stretching her legs, she felt a hard surface—the coffin itself. She now stood upon the iron casket of the vampire. More curious now than frightened, Maria knelt down to get a closer look at the writing on the casket. But the metal of the coffin was cracked, flaky, and apparently fragile. She had to work to maintain her balance, and once she did she held the candle toward the nameplate on the coffin. It was no use; like the coffin itself, the nameplate was rusted and nearly impossible to read.

Each year on Day of the Dead, Mexicans honor the memory of deceased loved ones by visiting their gravesites (pictured). One young girl's Day of the Dead visit in the early 1900s supposedly resulted in the reemergence of a vampire thought to have existed a century before.

Just then Maria felt something grab her leg. She screamed, bumped her head, shook her leg to get free, and climbed out of the tomb. She raced home without looking back. Still breathing heavily, she approached her front door. As she reached for the handle, she noticed the trail of blood running down her arm. She had bumped her head harder than she thought, and now she realized the blood had also stained the top part of her dress. Once inside, she locked the door. The house was just as she had left it: quiet and peaceful. She stopped the bleeding on her head, washed her dress, and slipped into bed, but she could not sleep. She was certain that the vampire would find her. He had tasted her blood and certainly hungered for more.

Fearing an Attack

The next day Maria tried to forget what had happened but found it impossible. Exhausted from lack of sleep, she struggled to get through the day. In bed that night she feared an attack, but after hours of restlessness she drifted into an uneasy slumber. She awoke in the early morning hours to find a dark figure looming over her bed. She screamed, but when her parents rushed into her room and turned on the light, the shadowy presence was gone. Overcome with fear, Maria confessed her nighttime excursion to the cemetery along with her encounter with El Vampiro. Her parents were frightened about their daughter's nocturnal wandering but laughed off her tales of the vampire. In fact, the doctor who treated her head wound also refused to believe her. Yet the next night the vampire returned. Her screams again brought her parents to her side. They noticed that the cut on her head had opened again, leaving a spot of blood on her pillow.

To calm her, Maria's mother slept in her daughter's room.

Strange as It Sounds...

Just like vampires themselves, people bitten by them may have an aversion to bright lights and garlic.

This went on for two nights. During this time, the wound showed no signs of healing, and Maria became weaker. On the third night Maria's mother soothed her daughter, lying with her until Maria fell asleep. Then she got up to use the bathroom, but upon returning she saw a dark figure hovering over her child's bed. She screamed and her husband rushed in, but again the figure was gone. Maria was also bleeding again. Maria's parents were now convinced that the vampire did indeed seek to destroy their daughter.

While not particularly religious, Maria's family now sought divine intervention. They called on a Pentecostal minister named Reverend Guivez, who came to the house and talked to the family about the beast terrorizing them. Before he left, Guivez anointed Maria's head wound and prayed with the family. During the prayers, a porcelain doll flew across the room and shattered against the wall directly above the reverend's head. Swallowing his own fear, Guivez shouted for the strange happenings to stop and for the evil entity affecting the young girl to leave the house. Instead cold air immediately filled the room, and the vampire suddenly appeared before the assembled people. Again the reverend demanded that the evil presence leave, invoking the name of Jesus Christ. From the other room the group heard the family cat screech. The feline dashed into the room, circling madly and crying out in anguish. Maria and her family took cover, fearing the cat might attack them. The frenzied animal then jumped through an open window and out into the street, where it was struck and killed by a passing car.

El Vampiro never again appeared. Soon after, Maria's head wound began healing normally, but she never again visited El Panteon de Belen. In time, life returned to normal, although Reverend Guivez's services became much in demand in the city.

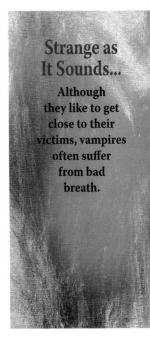

Strange as It Sounds...

Although they like to get close to their victims, vampires often suffer from bad breath.

Dom Augustin Calmet: Vampire Scholar

One of the first people to take a close and serious look at vampires and vampire attacks was the eighteenth-century Roman Catholic priest Dom Augustin Calmet. Born in Lorraine, France, Calmet studied at a Benedictine monastery and later taught philosophy and theology before writing a multivolume analysis of the Bible. Yet it is his 1746 study of vampire legends, folktales, eyewitness accounts, and newspaper reports for which he is most remembered today. Calmet investigated alleged attacks in eastern Europe and worked to understand the phenomenon, particularly as it related to Christian teachings in which blood—the blood of the crucified savior Jesus Christ—plays a primary role. Calmet was one of the earliest scholars to define vampires as undead beings who thrive on the blood of their victims; it was he who first described the common methods of destroying vampires. As to the question of whether vampires truly existed, Calmet appeared to waver. He reluctantly admitted that vampirism might be very real, saying, "It seems impossible not to subscribe to the belief which prevails . . . that these apparitions do actually come forth from the graves." But when critics chastised him for promoting superstition, Calmet agreed that little verifiable evidence of vampires existed.

Quoted in Anthony Masters, *The Natural History of the Vampire.* New York: Berkley Medallion, 1972, p. 85.

The Vampire with the Melodious Voice

As in Mexico, the vampire tradition is an ancient one in the Arab world. One story—nearly impossible to confirm—occurred in the fifteenth century in Baghdad, the capital city of present-day Iraq. An aging merchant expected to leave his only son his vast wealth when he died. He also wanted to see his child happy because he loved him dearly. To ensure the young man's future happiness, the old man conspired with an equally wealthy friend to arrange a marriage between the merchant's son and the friend's kind but plain daughter. After being shown a cameo, or portrait, of the daughter, the son, Abdul-Hassan, told his father he would consider marrying the young woman, but he needed time. Abdul-Hassan despised the idea of marrying a woman he did not love. He respected his father and held deep affection for the man who had raised him, but he foresaw a future of misery and unhappiness if he married someone he had never met.

As these thoughts troubled Abdul-Hassan's mind, he took a walk by the light of the moon. He strolled for hours along Baghdad's streets, and then wandered out into the country. It was then that he heard a voice—a beautiful, melodious voice—singing passages from the Koran, the Muslim holy book. The voice was accompanied by a strumming guitar. The gorgeous music stopped Abdul-Hassan in his tracks, and he realized now where it was coming from: a grove of orange trees. The young man made his way toward the sounds, following a path until he came to a modest home. On the balcony stood an alluring woman, but by the time Abdul-Hassan got close, she was gone.

He returned home, smitten with the beauty. The next day, after his morning prayers, he returned to the house, but no one was home. He talked to locals who knew the family and found out that the young woman was unmarried. Her father, brilliant put poor, could not afford to provide a dowry. But for Abdul-Hassan, that did not matter. He had found his true love, and he returned home to tell his father that the arranged marriage would never take place. Though disappointed, the old merchant could not refuse his son; he only wanted him to be happy.

A Graveyard Feast

Abdul-Hassan soon received permission to marry the beautiful woman whose dulcet tones so captivated him. Her name was Nadilla, and after the two young lovers were married, they settled into a blissful life. Then late one night Nadilla suddenly rose from bed and left the room. At first Abdul-Hassan thought nothing of it, but he waited for hours, and when she did return, in the hour before dawn, he pretended he was asleep. When Nadilla entered the room, he could see that she appeared frightened and confused. She said nothing of her absence, and the next night she disappeared again. This time her husband followed her. He stayed back so she would not see him, and after a time they came to a cemetery. Nadilla stopped at a large, open tomb; Abdul-Hassan watched in horror as his pretty young wife climbed in. He could not see any light coming from inside. He peered over the edge and inside saw a collection of pale and fanged creatures feasting on something he could not quite see. Suddenly he heard something coming, and he hid himself. This new creature was dragging a human corpse behind it. When the pale creature reached the tomb, it threw the cadaver in; the others immediately began drinking its fresh, still-warm blood. Nadilla joined them.

Amazed and deeply frightened by what he had seen,

Vampire Defense

According to an online organization called the Federal Vampire and Zombie Agency, the six rules of modern vampire self-defense are as follows:

1) **Stay Alert**

Because vampires often appear normal when in public, it is important to be on guard at all times, particularly after nightfall.

2) **Avoid Confined Areas**

Vampires like to roam in packs of two, three, or even four. Therefore, take precautions and avoid being backed into a corner or chased down an alley.

3) **Don't Run**

People can't outrun vampires.

4) **Do Not Go Quietly**

One of the best defenses against vampires is to shout or scream. This may scare them off.

5) **Don't Let Them See Fear**

Vampires are known for preying on the frail and weak. A person should be strong, assertive, and brave in their presence. The vampires may decide to look elsewhere for fresh plasma.

6) **Find a Doctor**

If attacked, a person should seek immediate medical attention. The vampire infects its victims through the bloodstream. Small cuts can be just as damaging as large ones.

Abdul-Hassan hurried home. The next night he asked his wife to join him at dinner, but she refused. It was then that he confronted her and told her what he had seen. Nadilla said nothing and only walked off silently to bed. In the middle of the night, once she thought he was sleeping, she attacked him, sitting on his chest and scratching at his neck, drawing blood. But Abdul-Hassan had only pretended to sleep. He fought off his vampire wife with a knife he had tucked under his pillow. She lunged at him, teeth bared, but he plunged the knife into her chest, killing her—or so he thought.

Three nights later, pale Nadilla rose from her grave and returned. The knife had done nothing. Abdul-Hassan had no choice but to flee. He returned in the daytime to the cemetery in which Nadilla was buried. Upon opening the coffin, he beheld his wife, rosy cheeked and smiling in her grave. He removed the corpse and burned it, scattering the ashes in the Tigris River.

An Ongoing Mystery

Vampire attacks obey no national or cultural boundaries. People from different cultures and backgrounds in countries around the globe claim to have been terrorized, touched, or bitten by the elusive beings known as vampires. Did these attacks really take place? And were the attackers truly vampires? The world may never know.

Chapter 4

Vampire Hunters

In the minds of many, vampires are the embodiment of evil. To destroy them, vampire hunters and slayers have traditionally been enlisted to identify and then root out the undead. Armed with holy water, crucifixes, garlic, and sharpened wooden stakes, these brave souls endanger their own lives to rid the world of an ancient curse.

It is not a job to be taken lightly, says a modern-day vampire hunter named Hellsinger: "If after your first successful destruction, you find you have a taste for the game, then maybe, you can join the ranks of the elite, but if you have any sense at all, you'll run and hide. Make no mistake about this, the only creature who is lonelier than the vampire, is the one who hunts it."[21] But while some purported hunters take the old-fashioned route, other, more scientifically minded, hunters search not for evidence of the supernatural but for logical explanations of mysterious phenomena.

Contemporary Vampire Hunter

Katherine Ramsland, a scholar and vampire investigator, takes the logical approach. She was bitten by the vampire bug as a child. The interest grew into a near obsession: She slept with her arms folded across her chest, as if dead, and told everyone she met that she was not really a child but a 403-year-old vampire. While many children outgrow an interest in the supernatural, Ramsland's thirst for all things fanged could not be satisfied.

As an adult she explored vampire subculture by enrolling in vampire classes, learning not only about the folklore surrounding the bloodsuckers but the habits of contemporary people who claim to be vampires. Before long, Ramsland made new friends who invited her to secret midnight parties, where revelers danced the night away but also drank each other's blood in modest amounts. She became familiar with the bloodsucking in-crowd of New York City's nightlife. But, thirsty only for knowledge, she wanted to know more. At one point she began receiving late-night phone calls from an anonymous blood drinker. When Ramsland requested a face-to-face interview to be used in a possible newspaper story, the mystery man refused. He told her that if they ever met, he might not be able to resist the urge to feast on her. Her lust for vampire lore and real-life encounters with the undead drove her on. Unlike vampires hunters in fiction, she did not want to harm her journalistic prey; she only wanted to learn the truth about their habits and bloody desires.

Her exploration took her to clubs not only in New York, but in Florida, which has a thriving, if secretive, vampire community. The clubs only proved to her that people that dress like vampires usually are not. Instead vampires typically avoid obvious displays of their vampirism. That way they are less likely to attract suspicion. Another misconception is that all vampires drink blood; Ramsland disputes this. "They will role-play it," she says, but "a lot of them are repulsed by it."[22] Those that do indulge first have the blood tested for diseases, and once it is deemed safe, drink it in what she refers to as "feeding circles." These take place not for nourishment but

Strange as It Sounds...

Vampires do not have reflections in mirrors.

for bonding, to make each member feel a part of the group. According to Ramsland, vampires are not so focused on blood, death, and darkness. Instead they have made a lifestyle choice that allows them to show themselves off: "Vampires are about beauty, sensuality. They'll go to great lengths to get perfect detail [in their clothing, makeup, and style]."[23]

Hunting the Highgate Vampire

Like Ramsland, vampire hunter Sean Manchester became obsessed with learning whether vampires truly existed. In 1967 he heard reports of vampirism at the Highgate Cemetery in London. There a schoolgirl named Elizabeth Wojdyla and her girlfriend told of seeing open graves and spirits rising from them. Furthermore, Wojdyla claimed that an evil spirit of some kind had tried to gain entrance to her bedroom.

Over the next couple of years, Manchester collected other, similar stories connected with Highgate. Then in 1969 Wojdyla complained of horrifying nightmares. This time, she said, the phantom entered her room. In the days and weeks that followed, she became sick with anemia, a condition in which a person's red blood cell count drops dramatically. Family members also noticed two distinct bite marks on her neck but feared authorities would not believe the fantastic story. With nowhere else to turn, Wojdyla's family called on Manchester, now a reputed vampire hunter, who, along with the young woman's boyfriend, transformed her room by placing crosses, garlic, and holy water around it. Wojdyla's health quickly improved, yet by this time more and more people were coming forward with vampire stories of their own.

Soon after the Wojdyla incident, dead dogs and cats, drained of blood, were discovered in the cemetery and an

Strange as It Sounds...

Eastern Europeans believe a vampire can be destroyed by cutting off its head and stuffing garlic into its mouth.

Highgate Cemetery (pictured) in London became the focus of a vampire investigation in the 1960s after a local girl reported seeing open graves and spirits at the cemetery. She later complained of a phantom entering her room at night—around the same time she developed anemia.

adjacent park. Evidence suggested that the animals were being used in bizarre rituals. When this story broke in the press, the vampire sightings were also revealed. The Highgate case turned into a media firestorm, as Londoners wondered whether a vampire was really stalking their neighborhoods.

Investigator Manchester received another report of a young woman with symptoms much like those of the now-cured Wojdyla. One night while the woman sleepwalked through the cemetery, Manchester followed her. She led him to a group of burial vaults and stopped. Manchester announced soon after that a vampire indeed haunted Highgate.

The episode reached an apparent climax when, in early 1970, Manchester and two helpers led hundreds of onlookers and a phalanx of news cameras into one of the cemetery's burial vaults and revealed three empty coffins, which they proceeded to strew with garlic and crosses. Things turned stranger and uglier later that year when vandals dug up the corpse of a young woman and attempted to burn it. Investigators concluded the vandals must have believed the body to be that of a vampire. Londoners were outraged at the incident and fearful that the bodies of their dead loved ones, too, could be mutilated. Police acted quickly, arresting two alleged vampire hunters and attempting to end the vampire frenzy.

Allegations of a Hoax

Manchester escaped suspicion of foul play until a competing vampire expert, David Farrant, claimed that the whole thing was a hoax. Years before, Farrant claimed he had seen the Highgate vampire but soon after was arrested for breaking into tombs in the cemetery. In 1978 he told the press he had made up the whole affair. Manchester denied any hoax and insisted he had been investigating the vampire long before Farrant. As if to bolster his case, Manchester revealed he had discovered a mysterious mansion near Highgate. After breaking in, he and his aides searched the premises and came upon a coffin in the basement. Inside was the vampire seen by Elizabeth Wojdyla 10 years before. The men dragged the coffin into the backyard, drove a stake through the vampire's heart, and burned the corpse and the coffin.

While Manchester claimed to have destroyed the vampire, by the early 1980s bloodless, dead animals were again found in the vicinity of the Highgate cemetery. Manchester drew the conclusion that this was the work of a victim of the first vampire. He called this bloodthirsty demon Lusia. After being awoken by dreams in which Lusia came to him, Manchester announced that the vampire was buried not in Highgate but in the Great Northern London Cemetery.

In 1982 Manchester sneaked into the graveyard, searching for Lusia's tomb. While there, he said, he was attacked by a cat-size spider that he quickly subdued with a stake through the heart. As dawn broke, the dead spider transformed into Lusia herself. Manchester found her grave and laid her body in the open tomb.

Much of the Highgate vampire story comes from Manchester himself, which he chronicled in a book about the adventure. Like Farrant, many remain skeptical about the events. "Despite all the hubbub," says writer Eric Nuzum, "no one ever did provide any proof that there was a Highgate vampire or that he had ever attacked anyone."[24] For his part, Manchester remains silent.

A Doomed Marriage

Definitive proof is even harder to find in the case of a nineteenth-century Russian vampire who challenged hunters like never before. Although little evidence exists today to prove the story, villagers who passed it down testified to its truth. In a small Russian province, the local governor fell in love with the daughter of one of his employees. The governor wooed the young woman, but he was a man of 60 and she was already betrothed to a handsome young soldier. None of this mattered to the governor, who was widely known as a cruel and tyrannical man. He insisted that his underling agree to the marriage and, fearing he would lose his job, the man did.

Yet the marriage appeared doomed from the start. The

Vampire Hunter's Detection Guide

The online site *The Vampire Hunter's Guide* and other sources suggest that hunters seeking confirmation of the existence of vampires should look for these signs:

At the Graveyard:
- Disturbed earth or coffins
- Broken crosses
- A trail of footprints leading from the grave
- Dogs refusing to enter the area
- No birds singing

Inside the Coffin:
- The corpse's eyes are open
- The body is bloated
- Fingernails and toenails are longer than is normal
- The body has not begun decomposition
- Dried or fresh blood around the corpse's mouth

governor was insanely jealous, and he chafed at any attention his new wife received from other men. He maintained control over his bride by screaming at her, beating her, and locking her in her room for weeks on end. She could not receive any visitors unless he was present. But the woman's imprisonment appeared to end when the governor suddenly fell sick. As he lay dying, he told her to swear a solemn oath never to marry again. At first she hesitated; she was, after all, still youthful and full of life. Only when he threatened to rise from the grave and kill her did she promise to remain chaste and forgo remarriage. The governor lingered for a few weeks, but he never recovered. His widow buried him in a cemetery across the river from their village.

Time passed; old promises were forgotten. And with the coming of spring, the governor's widow moved on with her life. She went about the business of maintaining her estate and managing her fortune. She attended the lavish parties of friends, and at one of them she was introduced to a former acquaintance: the handsome soldier with whom she had once been in love. The courtship moved quickly, and within two months she had remarried. The night of the wedding feast proceeded without incident until all were startled by wild shrieks coming from the bride's room. When a group of guests broke down her door, they found her nearly unconscious; outside they heard the sounds of a carriage speeding away.

On closer examination, a doctor found black and blue marks on her body and small, blood-red holes in her neck. "Upon recovering she stated that her deceased husband had suddenly entered her room," writes folklorist Raymond T. McNally, "appearing exactly as in life, with the exception of a dreadful pallor."[25]

The Vampire Escapes

Once she had recovered, the woman described her attacker. It was her dead husband, pale and fanged, and he had chided her for remarrying. Most who heard it that night discounted the fantastic tale. But the next morning the soldiers who guarded the bridge that spanned the river reported what they had seen the night before: a black coach pulled by six horses speeding toward the widow's mansion. The new governor ordered more soldiers to guard the bridge, but it mattered little. Each night, the dark coach, its horses blowing steam, somehow got past the guards and made its way into the courtyard of the mansion. Just before its arrival, all the members of the household would fall into a deep sleep, and every morning the widowed bride was found weak and bleeding, her life slowly ebbing away. Neither doctors nor priests could heal the woman nor stop the nightly intrusion.

In desperation, the governor stationed 50 soldiers at the bridge with orders to stop the interloper at all costs. Again the ghastly apparition of the dead man appeared. The soldiers shouted for him to stop, and a priest held out the crucifix to try and prevent the evil being from continuing. But suddenly an electric charge traveled through each of them, and they were momentarily paralyzed.

Finally the local archbishop insisted on a last resort. First, gravediggers exhumed the body. The corpse of the former governor was engorged with blood, nearly lifelike. Next the clergyman recited prayers over the body as a stake was driven through its heart. The Russian vampire never again rose from its grave; the widow thereafter lived in peace.

Destroying the Strigoi

Timothy Taylor does not believe that vampires can rise from graves. Yet the British archaeologist and cannibalism expert has made a name for himself by traveling the world and hunting for answers to ancient questions about death, ritual, and superstition. Taylor first visited Romania in the early 1980s, but it was on a return trip in 2004 that he came face-to-face with ancient tradition and its place in the modern world. He and a colleague, anthropologist Kathryn Denning, were there to film a documentary about the sources of Bram Stoker's novel *Dracula*, the most famous vampire story ever written. Taylor was already well versed in Romanian folklore. He knew of *strigoi* and *moroi*, restless spirits that rural Romanians believe rise from graves to haunt and terrorize the living. These vampire-like creatures can be created in a variety of ways; for example, if a person dies before marrying and a cat or bat leaps over the dead body before burial, or if a child's upper teeth grow in before the lower ones.

Upon arriving in eastern Europe, Taylor and Denning had been told about the case of Petre Toma, a hard-drinking family man who died in the village of Marotinu de Sus in 2003. His niece suspected him of being a *strigoi* because, she said, she had suffered from nightmares in which he came to her and feasted on her heart.

Taylor and Denning wanted to investigate this story further, so they visited Toma's grave with a Romanian anthropologist as a guide. The researchers learned that it is in the first 40 days after a person's death that he or she may develop into a *strigoi*, roaming the night in search of fresh blood. After this time period the *strigoi* becomes a *moroi*, able to search for fresh victims even during daylight hours.

As the three scientists looked for Toma's burial spot, they

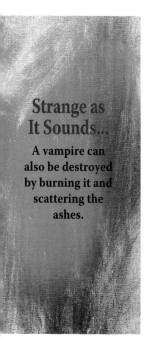

Strange as It Sounds...

A vampire can also be destroyed by burning it and scattering the ashes.

Rules of Vampire Hunting

According to the *LA Weekly*, a genuine vampire hunter submitted the following rules of vampire hunting:

Rule #1: Since a vampire is already dead it cannot be killed, only destroyed.

Rule #2: An annoyed vampire is a dangerous vampire.

Rule #3: Guns tend to annoy vampires. See rule #2.

Rule #4: Real vampires are evil.

Rule #5: Seduction by a vampire may lead to death or becoming a vampire.

Rule #6: (And this is the one that really counts.) Kill them all!

Rule #7: When in doubt, and all other times, execute rule #6.

Gendy Alimurung, "The Seven Rules of Vampire Hunting ...from a 'Real' Vampire Hunter," *LA Weekly* Blog, November 3, 2009. http://blogs.laweekly.com.

were confronted by an old man who waved a large scythe at them. It took a few minutes to calm 78-year-old Niculae Pedescu, but once they had, the old man described how the village vampire hunters had destroyed the *strigoi* Toma. At midnight they unearthed Toma's body, cut open his chest with a scythe, and removed his heart with a pitchfork. They carried the heart to a crossroads outside the village, where they roasted it, stuffed hot coals into the blood-collecting chambers called ventricles, and held it in the air. The wind blew flakes from the charred heart, and the men caught these in a small towel. They mixed the flakes with water and gave it to Toma's niece to drink, saying it would relieve her nightmares and put Toma's spirit to rest. At this point the niece's nightmares ended.

Hunting the Hunters

Like Taylor, Michael Bell knows all about vampires. Bell has spent the last decade digging into reports of vampirism and those who claimed to put the vampires to rest.

Bell has spent many hours looking at reports of mysterious deaths in Europe and the United States during the seventeenth and eighteenth centuries. During those centuries tuberculosis—a highly contagious and fatal respiratory disease—was common but not understood by most people. All they knew was that family members were getting sick and dying at a rapid rate. Physicians of the time often ordered exhumations to see whether someone had died of what were considered unnatural causes. If the face appeared rosy cheeked and the organs still contained fresh blood, vampirism was suspected. To prevent the corpse from rising again and feasting on innocent family members, doctors or local authorities would get to work, according to Bell:

They'd either cut out the heart or other organs and burn them to ashes, maybe feeding the ashes to people that were sick, or they'd just burn the entire corpse, and the sick family members would stand around the corpse and inhale the smoke. . . . That was how they stopped the vampires from finishing off the family.[26]

Other practices included turning a corpse upside down and reburying the body facedown or removing a leg or leg bone to prevent the reanimated corpse from walking. Where and how these methods of destruction came into being is unclear. Bell believes that Americans picked up on the vampire-killing techniques after reading about a wave of vampire attacks in the early seventeenth century in the country now known as Hungary.

The End of Vampire Hysteria

This period of vampire hysteria ended in the late nineteenth century as medical practice became more standardized and accepted in the United States. Superstition and the often strange medical solutions promoted by thousands of rural doctors receded. Scientific inquiry, with its emphasis on reason and deduction, became more widely accepted as a way of solving the mysteries surrounding sickness and death.

Embalming may also have convinced people that vampirism was little more than superstition. During the Civil War, when the bodies of slain soldiers had to be transported over many miles to their final resting place, bodily fluids were drained and replaced with special preservative chemicals—a new technique at the time. "Embalming basically disarms

Strange as It Sounds...
Some cultures believe that a person can be transformed into a vampire at birth if the child's mother did not eat enough salt during pregnancy.

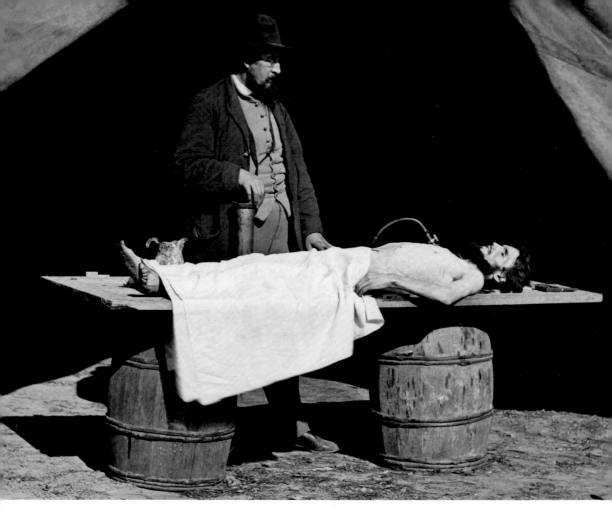

The body of a Union soldier undergoes the embalming process during the Civil War. This technique, which involves draining the body of all fluids and replacing them with preservative chemicals, may have contributed to a waning belief in vampires in the nineteenth century.

the corpse, like a bomb," Bell said. "You take the fuse out, it cannot become a vampire."[27]

Defusing the superstition surrounding vampires may not be as easy as Bell suggests. While cold, hard scientific facts may convince some people that actual vampires are little more than fiction, others will point to the bizarre and horrific crimes committed by those claiming to be vampires as proof of their bloody existence.

Chapter 5

Vampire Imitators

Modern science has undermined age-old superstitions about vampires and the occult. As science has slowly revealed more about the natural world, it has become clear to many that the idea of bloodsucking undead preying upon innocent and helpless victims is little more than fiction. Yet the twenty-first century has brought with it a new kind of vampirism. While most people today consider vampires little more than fictional fun, others take the matter seriously. This adoration of all things vampire goes far beyond simple interest in vampire books or movies. Instead such people will dress in black or have their teeth sharpened into fangs. Often referring to themselves as vampires, they gather for parties with others like themselves or perform dark rituals in which they drink blood in the privacy of their own homes.

While this kind of behavior strikes many as odd, these vampire imitators—human beings claiming to possess vampire-like powers—are typically peaceful and law-abiding. But in certain cases dabbling in vampirism turns deadly, as disturbed individuals use their self-proclaimed power to manipulate others and even commit brutal acts of murder.

Vampire Cults

Vampire cults are collections of like-minded people whose interest in vampirism can turn deadly. Typically composed of teens or young adults, these cults often attract those who feel like outsiders and are looking for a group or social circle that makes them feel as if they belong. Manuela Ruda became interested in vampirism in 1996 during a trip to Great Britain. There she spent time on the London club scene, where she met up with a group of people interested in vampires and Satanism, or devil worship. Before long her new friends coaxed her into drinking hot blood donated by group members. Ruda soon after began sleeping on graves and agreed to be buried once to see what it felt like. Upon returning home to Germany, Ruda also had two of her teeth pulled and replaced with fangs. She also persuaded her then boyfriend, Daniel Ruda, to behave like a vampire by staying up all night and sleeping in cemeteries.

Then in early 2001 Daniel had a vision: He saw the number 6667. (Some people think the number 666 is a sign of the devil.) This, Daniel believed, meant the two should marry on June 6, or 6/6, and kill themselves a month later, after performing a ritualistic killing. Their victim, Frank Hackerts, was a friend. He worked in an auto parts store. The Rudas invited Hackerts to their home on July 6 for a party, but when he arrived they stabbed him to death. At the trial, Manuela and Daniel pleaded not guilty. Manuela claimed that Satan had forced her hand. In a written statement, she said, "We are not murderers. It was the execution of an order. Satan ordered it. We had to obey."[28]

Their ghoulish behavior aside, little evidence exists to suggest that the Rudas were truly vampires. What is apparent to many sociologists and psychologists is that those who join vampire cults often become involved because they feel alienated. Vulnerable and easily influenced by others in the group, these so-called vampires become confused and more willing to participate in strange, often harmful, behavior. According to one clinical case study, "At the core of vampire cult activity are a series of games and rituals that include bloodletting, sacrifice . . . and drugs in which the membership engage."[29]

Vampire Murder in Florida

Rod Ferrell was another troubled teen, and from an early age he learned how to influence and manipulate others. He grew up in an abusive household in Murray, Kentucky, and spent his early teens drifting into gangs and drug use. His mother joined a vampire cult, and soon her son did, too. At 16, Ferrell and his friends began calling their close-knit group the Vampire Clan and dabbling in Satanic worship. Locals suspected them of breaking into an animal shelter and killing 2 puppies. Ferrell bragged to anyone who would listen that he was a 500-year-old vampire named Vesago. He

Manuela Ruda, charged with the murder of a friend, enters a German courtroom in 2002. Ruda and her boyfriend engaged in bizarre rituals such as drinking heated blood and sleeping on graves. Ruda also replaced two of her teeth with fangs.

became involved with 15-year-old Heather Wendorf from Eustis, Florida. Wendorf wanted to join the clan, but her parents, Richard Wendorf and Naoma Queen, were making it difficult. Finally she asked Ferrell to help steal her parents SUV so she could run away with him.

That was all Ferrell needed to hear. On November 25, 1996, he and his friend Scott Anderson drove to Eustis and met Wendorf. Ferrell and Wendorf walked to a local cemetery, where they cut their skin and drank each other's blood because Wendorf wanted to become a vampire like Ferrell. After the ritual, Ferrell and Anderson sent Wendorf away to a friend's house. The two young men then drove to Wendorf's parents' house and entered through the unlocked garage door, picking up a crowbar they found inside. Finding Richard Wendorf on the couch asleep, Ferrell bludgeoned him with the crowbar, killing him. Moments later, Naoma Queen came upon Ferrell and Anderson. She fought her attackers, throwing hot coffee at them, but she, too, was beaten to death.

After the bloody deed Ferrell and Anderson picked up Heather Wendorf and two others and drove west in the Wendorfs' SUV. Ferrell's favorite video arcade, located in Baton Rouge, Louisiana, was the destination. For four days the group eluded capture, but they needed money. In desperation, Charity Keesee, one of the clan members, phoned her mother in South Dakota to ask for cash. Keesee's mother contacted police, who tricked the group into meeting at a Baton Rouge hotel, where they were arrested. Despite being surprised, Ferrell bragged about the murders to law enforcement. The Vampire Clan was jailed for a week in Louisiana before being sent back to Florida.

In February 1998 Ferrell pleaded guilty to two counts of

premeditated, first-degree murder, calling Anderson an accessory and the others completely innocent. Lake County circuit judge Jerry Lockett sentenced Ferrell to death in Florida's electric chair, calling him "a disturbed young man" who proves "there is genuine evil in the world."[30] Ferrell, the self-proclaimed vampire, was to become one of the youngest Americans ever executed. But in September 1999 the Florida Supreme Court reduced the sentence to life imprisonment without the possibility of parole.

Vampire Killing: Welsh Teen Murders Neighbor

Although not part of a cult, Matthew Hardman exhibited some, but not all, of the traits of a traditional vampire. Hardman, a Welsh paperboy and high school student, appeared normal to neighbors and friends. He lived quietly with his mother and her partner in England. His parents had separated when the boy was 13; that same year his father died of a heart attack. Over the next four years, Hardman developed an interest, glancing at first, in vampires and the occult. He surfed the Internet for hours, quickly becoming obsessed not only with the concept of vampirism but with a quest to find real vampires.

Finally, after much searching, he believed he had found one. She was a 16-year-old German girl, and her pale skin and dark hair convinced him that she was one of the undead. Hardman, now 17, was so certain the girl was a vampire that he finally got up the nerve and told her so. She did not understand what he was talking about, but Hardman told her not to fear. He would keep her secret, but he asked her to bite his neck and make him a vampire, too. He got close enough to her that he tried to press his neck against her lips. The girl screamed and called for help; Hardman fled.

Strange as It Sounds...

While holy water typically burns a vampire, it does not typically destroy it.

But the incident did not deter him. He convinced himself that he did not need the German girl in order to become a vampire. Instead he would prove his worth without her. In November 2001 Hardman broke into the north Wales home of his neighbor, 90-year-old Mabel Leyshon. The woman was watching television at the time. He stabbed her 22 times with a kitchen knife, removed her heart, and wrapped it in newspaper, after which he put it in a saucepan and laid it on top of a silver platter. At Leyshon's feet he placed two fireplace pokers in the shape of a cross. The bizarre ritual ended when he drank her blood in an apparent attempt to turn himself into a vampire. Hardman had been the woman's paperboy.

Police investigators quickly zeroed in on Hardman—his odd behavior at school, his obsession with demons, vampires, and dark rituals. They also traced the murder weapon back to the Hardman home. During his trial, prosecutors vividly described a disturbed young man who had bragged to friends that he was going to find a way to live forever. After hearing the evidence, the jury deliberated for four hours before returning a unanimous decision: guilty. Hardman received a 12-year prison sentence. During sentencing, the judge scolded Hardman, describing his crimes as "carefully calculated. You had hoped for immortality," he said. "All you achieved was to brutally end another person's life."[31]

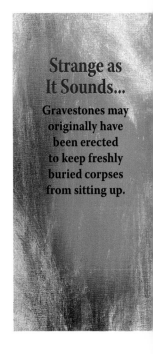

Strange as It Sounds...

Gravestones may originally have been erected to keep freshly buried corpses from sitting up.

The Vampire of London

Unlike Hardman, Londoner John George Haigh, born in 1909, was steeped in religion from an early age. His parents were members of a fundamentalist Protestant group known as the Plymouth Brethren. They raised their son with a respect, even reverence, for the image of Jesus Christ's death on the cross and his holy blood.

Warm-Weather Vampires

Vampires in southern Florida have long tried to fly—like bats—under the proverbial radar. Preferring the term *vampyres*, to draw a distinction between themselves and the fictional variety, these bloodsuckers attend parties, hang out, and post messages in chat rooms. They also really drink blood. But instead of murdering innocents, they obtain their supply from volunteers known as black swans. Typically the process goes something like this: A black swan exposes an arm or a fleshy thigh. Then a vampyre takes a sharp knife or scalpel and makes a slit, careful to cut lightly and at just the right angle so as not to leave a scar. Once a small bit of blood is delicately drained the vampyre takes a modest drink. Consumers of the blood say it replenishes their energy. But the blood-craving Floridians are quick to point out that they are not to be feared. "It's not Satanism, and we are not evil," says Evan Christopher, host of the Vampire Gathering, a monthly meeting in Tampa. "There are a lot of us out there—some people don't even realize they are vampires. We're here to offer advice and to tell these kids, 'You are not alone.'"

Quoted in Michael J. Mooney, "South Florida's Underground Vampires Lust for More than Your Heart," *New Times*, February 5, 2009. www.browardpalmbeach.com.

Their religious obsession also led them to force their son to live in a small pen set up in the garden behind the family house. With little engagement with the outside world, the boy grew into a disturbed young man who began having religious visions. One, he said, told him to drink his own urine. Another showed him a forest of crosses that became trees dripping with blood. In this recurring vision a man collected the blood in a bowl and offered it to a thirsty Haigh, who drank it. Haigh interpreted this dream as a signal that he needed blood to survive.

On the surface, Haigh appeared normal—well groomed, quiet, and nattily dressed. He married in 1934 and began work, first in insurance and then in advertising. But soon after, he was arrested and jailed for stealing, and his marriage ended in divorce. Then, after pretending to be a lawyer, Haigh was jailed again.

While in prison he planned what he deemed the perfect murder, and upon his release he went about constructing a laboratory in a small workshop he rented. In 1944 Haigh killed a former employer, William McSwan, the wealthy owner of an amusement park. Three years later he lured Archibald and Rose Henderson to his laboratory and shot them before draining their blood and dissolving their cadavers in a huge vat of sulfuric acid in order to hide the evidence. He also stole their jewelry and money.

After Haigh murdered his neighbor Olive Durand-Deacon in 1949 and tried to pawn her fur coat, police arrested him. Haigh was confident he would be acquitted because he was certain police would never discover a body. But when asked about his deeds, Haigh told detective inspector Albert Webb that "if I told you the truth, you would not believe me. It sounds too fantastic to believe."[32]

Detectives found the fantastic all too real once they entered Haigh's lab. Among the horrors they found were various body parts, including teeth, all remnants of Haigh's diabolical work. Fearing the court had the evidence it needed against him, Haigh confessed to killing nine people and told authorities that he drank the blood of his victims. Subsequently the press dubbed him the Vampire of London. But according to vampire investigator Katherine Ramsland, Haigh's blood-drinking story was probably not true and only served as part of his larger plan to make officials think him insane. According to Ramsland, "His claim to be a vampire in need of human blood was most likely the result of a wish to present the most shocking case he could think of. It was simply a way to avoid the death penalty."[33] If this was the killer's plan, it failed. A jury quickly found Haigh guilty and sentenced him to death. He went to the gallows on August 10, 1949.

San Francisco Nights

Such real-life horror stories give vampires a bad name, at least according to members of San Francisco's vampire community. Neither part of a cult nor composed of homicidal maniacs, these "real" vampires spend their leisure time hanging out at Bay Area clubs that cater to like-minded clientele.

Cole and Rhiannon met at just such a San Francisco club known as the Glass Cat during a vampire ball. Now close friends, both typically dress in black. Cole says that like many people, his first experience with vampirism came from movies. Only later did he discover that being a vampire had little to do with Hollywood portrayals. Instead vampirism has more to do with energy than with rising from crypts,

Attacks in Italy

Between 1867 and 1871 a reputed vampire terrorized a small Italian village. His victims included 14-year-old Johanna Motta, violently murdered while traveling to a nearby village. Maria Previtali, 19, had heard about Motta and often laid awake thinking about the bloody crime. She also knew of a neighbor, Mrs. Frigeni, who had been attacked and drained of blood on her way to work in the fields. Previtali, too, worked in the fields, and as she returned one evening, she heard footsteps behind her. She walked faster, hoping she might lose her pursuer, but the more quickly she moved, the more quickly he moved. This continued for nearly 10 minutes before Previtali, exhausted and frightened, tripped on a stone. As she fell, she felt 2 hands grasping at her neck and dragging her to the ground. She kicked at her attacker and landed a blow to the stomach. The man doubled over in pain. Previtali now saw the vampire's face. It was her cousin, 22-year-old Vincent Verzini. Previtali dashed home and reported the attack. Verzini was subsequently arrested and sentenced to life in prison. Verzini admitted to having no supernatural powers. Instead he said, "I had an unspeakable delight in strangling women. . . . It satisfied me to seize [them] by the neck and suck their blood."

Quoted in Brad Steiger, *Real Vampires: Night Stalkers and Creatures from the Darkside*. Detroit: Visible Ink, 2010, p. 22.

According to one vampire aficionado, San Francisco's Nob Hill (pictured) is a hotspot for vampire activity.

shunning garlic, and avoiding wooden stakes. Calling it a biodeficiency syndrome, Cole is certain that vampires are simply people lacking in energy, or life force. Since their own bodies are relatively weak, vampires seek outside sources of power. Although he admits to drinking two or three teaspoons of blood from time to time, he insists that other vampires may attend a loud concert or move through a large crowd to "suck up" the required energy. Rhiannon agrees, calling vampires "energy absorbers."[34] By simply touching a volunteer for 30 seconds to a minute, she says she and Cole are able to fulfill their needs.

Like Rhiannon and Cole, Kitty Burns has long been attracted to all things vampire. She also rejects the violence often associated with vampire imitators and vampire cults. Instead she enjoys the trappings of vampirism—the black clothes, the dark eyeliner, the red lipstick, the pale skin— and seeks to share her fascination.

In 2004 Burns created the Vampire Tour of San Francisco, during which she leads people to some of the city's purported vampire hot spots. Once the tour begins, Burns becomes Mina Harker, a character from the novel *Dracula*, and asks her tourists to follow behind her lit candle. She takes her followers to Grace Cathedral, which she claims the city's vampires tried to burn down more than once; Nob Hill, a notorious vampire neighborhood; and the Fairmont Hotel, where past murder and mayhem have convinced her that vampires roam the corridors.

City officials consider Burns's vampire tour a harmless tourist attraction. The dividing line between harmless, fun-loving vampire imitators and destructive, murderous ones is extreme. Vampire folklore, fashion, and behavior have inspired generations of people to imagine a world in which good does not always triumph over evil and where the forces of darkness are powerful and exciting. Encounters with vampires, real or imagined, will likely continue. But the truth about vampires might well remain a mystery.

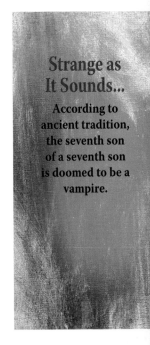

Strange as It Sounds...

According to ancient tradition, the seventh son of a seventh son is doomed to be a vampire.

Source Notes

Introduction: "Vampires Will Always Be with Us"

1. Quoted in Otto Penzler, ed., *The Vampire Archives*. New York: Vintage Crime/Black Lizard, 2009, p. xvi.

Chapter 1: Searching for Clues

2. Quoted in Mireya Navarro, "Animals Killed, an Island Is Abuzz," *New York Times*, January 26, 1996. www.nytimes.com.
3. Quoted in Navarro, "Animals Killed, an Island Is Abuzz."
4. Quoted in Navarro, "Animals Killed, an Island Is Abuzz."
5. Quoted in Paul Barber, *Vampires, Burial, and Death: Folklore and Reality.* New Haven, CT: Yale University Press, 1988, p. 20.
6. Raymond T. McNally, *A Clutch of Vampires.* Greenwich, CT: New York Graphic Society, 1974, p. 55.
7. McNally, *A Clutch of Vampires*, p. 49.
8. Quoted in Dudley Wright, *The Book of Vampires.* New York: Causeway, 1973, p. 180.
9. Quoted in Wright, *The Book of Vampires*, p. 181.
10. Quoted in Penzler, *The Vampire Archives*, p. 180.
11. Quoted in Katherine Ramsland, *The Science of Vampires.* New York: Berkley, 2002, p. 17.
12. Quoted in Jeff Belanger, "Mercy Brown, the Rhode Island Vampire," Ghost Village, June 14, 2003. www.ghostvillage.com.
13. Quoted in Belanger, "Mercy Brown, the Rhode Island Vampire."
14. Quoted in Barber, *Vampires, Burial, and Death*, p. 100.
15. Philip M. Boffey, "Rare Disease Proposed as Cause for 'Vampires,'" *New York Times*, May 31, 1985. www.nytimes.com.

Chapter 2: Vampire Sightings

16. Quoted in Brad Steiger, *Real Vampires: Night Stalkers and Creatures from the Darkside.* Detroit: Visible Ink, 2010, p. 27.
17. Lara, "Your True Tales," About.com: Paranormal Phenomena, July 2003. http://paranormal.about.com.
18. Quoted in Steiger, *Real Vampires*, p. 182.
19. Quoted in Steiger, *Real Vampires*, p. 183.

Chapter 3: Vampire Attacks

20. J. Gordon Melton, *The Vampire Book.* Detroit: Visible Ink, 1999, p. 35.

Chapter 4: Vampire Hunters

21. Quoted in Gendy Alimurung, "The Seven Rules of Vampire Hunting . . . from a 'Real' Vampire Hunter," *LA Weekly* Blog, November 3, 2009. http://blogs.laweekly.com.
22. Quoted in Liz Langley, "Interview with the Vampire Hunter," *Orlando (FL) Weekly*, October 28, 1998. www.orlandoweekly.com.
23. Quoted in Langley, "Interview with the Vampire Hunter."
24. Eric Nuzum, *The Dead Travel Fast:*

Stalking Vampires from Nosferatu to Count Chocula. New York: Macmillan, 2007, p. 126.

25. McNally, *A Clutch of Vampires*, p. 187.

26. Quoted in Matthew Derby, "Michael Bell," *Believer*, October 2004. www.believermag.com.

27. Quoted in Derby, "Michael Bell."

Chapter 5: Vampire Imitators

28. Quoted in Charles P. Wallace, "The Devil Made Us Do It," *Time*, January 28, 2002. www.time.com.

29. Thomas W. Miller et al., "An Adolescent Vampire Cult in Rural America: Clinical Issues and Case Study," *Child Psychiatry and Human Development*, 1999, p. 211.

30. Quoted in Donald P. Baker, "17-Year-Old Sentenced to Die in Fla.; Penalty for Young 'Vampire' Murderer Part of National Trend," *Washington Post*, February 28, 1998, p. A03.

31. Quoted in BBC News, "Teenager Guilty of 'Vampire' Murder," August 2, 2002. http://news.bbc.co.uk.

32. Quoted in Max Haines, *True Crime Stories*. New York: Barnes and Noble, 2003, p. 186.

33. Ramsland, *The Science of Vampires*, p. 109.

34. Quoted in Steiger, *Real Vampires*, p. 132.

For Further Exploration

Books

Michelle Belanger, ed., *Vampires in Their Own Words: An Anthology of Vampire Voices*. Woodbury, MN: Llewellyn, 2007.

Angela Cybulski, ed., *Vampires: Fact or Fiction?* San Diego, CA: Greenhaven, 2003.

William Patrick Day, *Vampire Legends in Contemporary American Culture: What Becomes a Legend Most*. Lexington: University of Kentucky Press, 2009.

Stuart A. Kallen, *Vampires*. San Diego, CA: ReferencePoint, 2008.

Otto Penzler, ed., *The Vampire Archives*. New York: Vintage Crime/Black Lizard, 2009.

Katherine Ramsland, *The Science of Vampires*. New York: Berkley, 2002.

Web Sites

Dracula's Homepage (www.ucs.mun.ca/~emiller). Aspiring vampire scholars might want to check out this Web site, maintained by internationally renowned *Dracula* expert and folklorist Elizabeth Miller. Read the entire novel or click through novelist Bram Stoker's notes for his legendary book. Also included is information on Vlad the Impaler, one of the models for Dracula himself.

Ghost Story (www.ghost-story.co.uk). This well-organized and exhaustive site is chock-full of information on the macabre, including the story of the Highgate vampire, as well as stories and photos of ghosts and haunted castles and churches.

Staking Claims: The Vampires of Folklore and Fiction, Committee for Skeptical Inquiry (www.csicop.org/si/show/staking_claims_the_vampires_of_folklore_and_fiction). A well-researched article by Paul Barber about the reality of Vlad Dracula and how myths and legends commonly associated with him have distorted the historical record.

Vampire, the Skeptic's Dictionary (www.skepdic.com/vampires.html). A site maintained by a renowned skeptic who questions the validity of vampire beliefs and provides links to related subjects.

Vampire Website (www.vampirewebsite.net). Its tagline, "It's time to emerge," suggests that real vampires are out there. But much of the site simply contains interesting information about the ongoing vampire phenomenon, including a selection of vampire jokes and vampire myths and facts.

Vampires (www.vampires.com). This site is a vampire newsmagazine and directory covering popular games, stories, pictures, and books, including *Twilight*, *True Blood*, and *Vampire Diaries*.

Index

Note: Page numbers in boldface refer to illustrations.

A

Abdul-Hassan, 43–44, 46
Ana, 27–28
Anderson, Scott, 64, 66
animal killings
    by chupacabras, 9, 21
    in Highgate Cemetery, 49–50, 51
Austria, 15

B

Baghdad, 43–44, 46
banishment of vampires, 41
Bathory, Countess Elizabeth, 33, 35–36
bats, 5, **6**, 56
belief in vampires, 4, 5
Bell, Michael E.
    on embalming, 59–60
    on Mercy Brown, 18
    on preventing future attacks, 58–59
    on wasting diseases and vampirism, 16
biodeficiency syndrome, 72–73
black swans, 68
Boffey, Philip M., 20
breath of vampires, 41
Brown, Edwin, 16
Brown, Mercy, 16, 18
Bulgaria, 4
Bundy, Ted, 24
Burns, Kitty, 73

C

Calmet, Dom Augustin, 42
Carniola (Slovenia), 13
Carol, 30–32
cemeteries, **39**

Baghdad, 44, 46
    gravestones, 67
    Great Northern London, 52
    Highgate, 49–52, **50**
    Panteon de Belen, El, 37–38, 40
    signs of vampires in, 53
characteristics of vampires
    absence of reflection, 48
    bad breath, 41
    hairy palms, 46
    non–blood drinking, 48–49
chiang shih, 5
children, encounters with vampires by
    Carol, 30–32
    Lara, 25, 27–28
    Maria, 37–38, 40–41
Chile, chupacabras in, 21
China
    chupacabras, **10**
    kiang shi (chiang shih) in ancient, 4–5
Christianity
    banishment of vampires, 41
    holy water, 66
    obsession with, 67, 69
    prayers to destroy vampires, 55
    Saint-Germain and Jesus, 22
    teachings about blood, 42
    vampires and churches, 62
Christopher, Evan, 68
chupacabras, 8–9, **10**, 21
Cole, 70, 72, 73
consumption (illness), 16, **17**, 58
Cranswell, Amelia, 24–25
Cranswell, Edward, 24–25
Cranswell, Michael, 24–25
Croglin Grange, 24–25
cults, vampire
    activities of, 63–66

definition of, 62
in Florida, 68
Satan and, 62, 63, 68

D
Day of the Dead, 37, **39**
defenses against vampires, 45
demons
    epilepsy and, 33
    worship of, 62, 63
Denning, Kathryn, 56, 58
destruction of vampires
    boiling head, 70
    burning organs/corpses, 25, 46, 56, 59
    decapitation and garlic, 49
    dousing with holy water, 15
    hunter's kit contents, 54
    prayers for, 55
    rules for, 57
    stake through heart, 52, 55
Dolphin, David H., 18, 20
Dracula (Stoker), 4
Durand-Deacon, Olive, 69

E
embalming, 59–60, **60**
England
    Croglin Grange, 24–25
    Great Northern London Cemetery, 52
    Highgate Cemetery, 49–52, **50**
epilepsy and demonic possession, 33
evidence of vampirism
    chupacabras, 8–9, **10**
    in Great Britain, criminal, 49–52,
        62–63, 66–67, 69–70
    in Hungary, 11
    in India, 14
    in Italy, criminal, 71
  in Mexico, 37–38
    in Slovenia, 13
    symptoms of illnesses, 15–16, **17**, 18, 20,
        58

F
Farrant, David, 51
Federal Vampire and Zombie Agency, 45
Ferrell, Rod, 63–64, 66
flying foxes, **6**

G
Gaiman, Neil, 7
Garcia, Hector J., 9
garlic, 20, 49
gender
    belief in vampires and, 4, 5
    percent of vampires by, 7
George III (king of England), 20
Grando, 13
gravestones, reason for, 67
Great Northern London Cemetery, 52
Greece, 4
Guadalajara, 37–38
Guadalupe, Luis, 8–9
Guivez, Reverend, 41

H
Hackerts, Frank, 62
Haigh, John George, 67, 69–70
Hardman, Mathew, 66–67
Helsinger, 47
Henderson, Archibald, 69
Henderson, Rose, 69
Highgate Cemetery, 49–52, **50**
holy water, 15, 66
Hungary, 11, 33, 35–36
hysteria and superstition, end of, 59–60

I
illnesses
    porphyria, 18, 20
    rabies, 18
    wasting/consumption, 15–16, **17**, 58
immortality, 12, 21
    See also destruction of vampires
India, 14

intelligence of vampires, 32
Iran, 29
Iraq, 43–44, 46
Italy, 71

J
Joo, Ilona, 35

K
Kaplan, Steven, 26
Kenya, 5
kiang shi, 5
Kordiyeh, Ali Reza Khoshruy, 29

L
langsuyars, 19
Lara, 25, 27–28
LA Weekly (magazine), 57
legends, 4–5
Leyshon, Mabel, 67
Luisa, 52

M
Majorova, Erzsi, 36
Malaysia, 19
Manchester, Sean, 49–52
Maria, 37–38, 40–41
Marie Antoinette (queen of France), 22
Mau Mau, 5
McNally, Raymond T.
    on Grando, 13
    on Paole, 11
    on Russian vampire, 54
McSwan, William, 69
Melton, J. Gordon, 35
Mexico, 37–38, **39**, 40–41
Meyer, Stephenie, 5
mirrors, 48
moroi, 56, 58
Motta, Johanna, 71

N
Nadasdy, Count Ferenc, 35
Nadilla, 44, 46
Native American beliefs, 4
New England (U.S.), 15–16
New York City, 28, 30
Nosferatu (movie), 16, **17**

O
Occult Review (magazine), 13

P
Panteon de Belen, El, 37–38, 40
Paole, Arnold, 11
Pedescu, Niculae, 58
porphyria, 18, 20
prevention of attacks, 45
    See also destruction of vampires
Previtali, Maria, 71
psychic vampires, 9
Puerto Rico, 8–9

Q
Queen, Naoma, 64

R
rabies, 18
Ramsland, Katherine, 47–49, 70
Rhiannon, 70, 73
Rhode Island, 16
Romania, 56, 58
Ruda, Daniel, 62
Ruda, Manuela, 62, **63**
Russia, 52, 54–55

S
Saint-Germain, Count de, 21–22
salt, 59
San Francisco, 70, 72–73, **72**
sanguine vampires, definition of, 14
Satan and vampire cults, 62, 63, 68
seventh sons, 73

Slovenia, 13
Soto, José, 9
Steiger, Brad, 22
Stoker, Bram, 4
strigoi, 56, 58
symptoms of victims, 13–15, 16, 36, 37, 40

T
Taylor, Timothy, 56, 58
Tehran Vampire, 29
Temple of the Vampire, 12
Thorko, 35
Toma, Petre, 56, 58
Transylvania, **34**
tuberculosis, 16, **17**, 58
Twilight series, 5, 7

U
United States, encounters in
 Carol's, 30–32
 New England, 15–16, 18
 New York, 28, 30
 San Francisco, 70, 72–73, **72**
ustrel, 4

V
Vampire Bible, 12
Vampire Clan, 63–64
vampire communities, 26, 70, 72–73
 See also cults, vampire
Vampire Gathering, 68
Vampire Hunter's Guide, The (Web site), 53
Vampire Research Center, 26
vampires
 average female, 28
 average male, 25
 becoming, 12
 categories of, 26
 IQs of, 32
Vampire Tour of San Francisco, 73
Vampiro, El, 37–38
vampyres, 68
Vardalek, Count, 15
Verzini, Vincent, 71
Vesago, 63

W
wasting illnesses, 15–16, **17**, 58
Wendorf, Heather, 64
Wendorf, Richard, 64
Wojdyla, Elizabeth, 49, 51